SHOW UP²¹

5 Practical Ways to Activate Your Leadership and Rise to the Challenge

A *First Lead Yourself* companion

By Stacey Ashley

First published in 2021 by Stacey Ashley
© Stacey Ashley
The moral rights of the author have been asserted.

Author:	
	Stacey Ashley
Title:	
	SHOW UP[21]: 5 practical ways to activate your leadership and rise to the challenge. A First Lead Yourself companion
ISBN:	
	978-0-6451006-0-0 (pbk) 978-0-6451006-1-7 (ebook)
Subjects:	
	Business, Leadership, Executive Coaching, Leadership Coaching

Editor: Dalida Boustead
Cover design and typeset: BookPOD

Disclaimer:
The material in this publication is of the nature of general comment only, and does not represent professional advice. It is not intended to provide specific guidance for particular circumstances and it should not be relied on as the basis for any decision to take action or not take action on any matter which it covers. Readers should obtain professional advice where appropriate, before making any such decision. To the maximum extent permitted by law, the author and publisher disclaim all responsibility and liability to any person, arising directly or indirectly from any person taking or not taking action based on the information in this publication.

Also by Stacey Ashley
The New Leader
First Lead Yourself

DEDICATION

To every leader who is showing up

What People Are Saying About Stacey Ashley

Your session was enriching, practical and truly effective in providing possibilities for transformation. Your translation of complex concepts into easy and doable tips is simply brilliant. I think filling our cups, fostering connection, elevating our practice and operating in our zone of genius are illuminating and inspirational thoughts that will help us face up, show up and step up to a better 2021. Once again, thanks a ton for sharing your expertise and giving us your valuable time. Your presence and contributions to APAC are precious and much appreciated.

Dr Ann Dolly, President, APAC

The Asia Pacific Alliance of Coaches (APAC) had the absolute joy of Stacey Ashley as one of our esteemed speakers at the recent APAC Coaching Fiesta on 6 December 2020. Stacey shared on Leading Possibilities, giving coaches and leaders very practical principles and frameworks to lead their tribes forward. Stacey was professional and suave, a role model in what she preaches. I highly recommend her as a speaker and mentor to leaders.

Irene Chia PCC, Executive Director & OD Coach

The BEING of leadership is never spoken about! Thank you for writing on this! *First Lead Yourself* is a brilliant book that actually addresses the BEING and embodiment of leadership. This topic is so often missed in leadership books. I am so glad Stacey wrote this book because it has really uplevelled my leadership ability.

Dave Thompson, Founder of Inspirational Book Writers

I have worked with Stacey over many years, in various capacities. Stacey is a consummate professional, experienced executive coach, trainer and mentor. Stacey is highly regarded for her expertise in the leadership and coaching profession and brings great depth, insight and heart to all she does. If you are lucky enough to work with Stacey, you will be forever changed for the better!

Tracey McMenamin, Director People & Culture at NT Government

I have had the privilege to work directly for Stacey and now see her having developed a successful career as a thought leader, coach and mentor in leadership. She is a very strong and thoughtful leader who was able to empower people of diverse backgrounds and bring out the best in them. It is no surprise to see her translate that into an ability to help thousands of aspiring and experienced leaders reach their maximum potential. An inspiring career.

Bob Buiaroski, Head of Global Client COO's at State Street

Stacey comes with a rare combination of great subject matter expertise and amazing ability to connect with people. Her clarity on topics like leadership, coaching and managing change is extraordinary. Along with it she is always ready to go the extra mile to ensure her clients get lots of value and elevate themselves. I wish Stacey tremendous success in all that she undertakes. Her work is highly recommended.

Hima Pravin, Founder at Meraqi Consulting

Stacey is an extraordinary coach and facilitator. She takes the room on a journey with great energy and conviction, while her stories (both relatable and inspiring) build more credibility with every passing minute. Stacey truly leads people to a place where they're comfortable making great decisions. Thanks so much, Stacey. I'll work with you again at every opportunity.

**Cath Nolan, Leadership &
Diversity Coach at Gender Gap Gone**

She is an engaging speaker, adept at encouraging audience participation and able to roll with the flow of an event. She is energetic and insightful, and uses real life examples to ensure the content is relevant and meaningful for the audience. We would be delighted to work with her again.

Stephanie Campanale, Executive Producer at Key Media

CONTENTS

INTRODUCTION

I had intended to write my next book this January. Yet the book I had planned to write didn't feel right. And so I chose not to do it yet.

Instead I have found myself writing an altogether different book. There was no plan to write this particular book at all. It really came out of the blue. A spur of the moment decision in the middle of a conversation with some colleagues and one of my mentors.

You see, I had in my mind that all my books needed to be of a certain size and style. Yet when my mentor held up a small book as an example of one of the different styles of book an author can create for their audience, and said, 'You can always write a book like this,' the penny dropped.

I have been speaking at a number of global events recently, and the particular focus of these talks had garnered such strong responses that I realised I needed to turn these ideas into a book. Quickly. The ideas are so relevant and needed by leaders right now.

I have been speaking about some of the concepts related to my most recent book, *First Lead Yourself*. The focus was how to support yourself as a leader in a sustainable way, despite the conditions that you might be operating in. As we know, the last year, 2020, has certainly had its fair share of challenges for leaders. And while most leaders have responded admirably, they have only just begun to realise that this is the beginning of a really significant marathon of leadership. That we have a long way to go until we settle into the new way of the world, following the transformation that was initiated by the COVID-19 pandemic. And that can feel daunting.

I first spoke about this at the World Coaching Congress in October 2020. And then I was invited to speak at a number of other events, including the Asia Pacific Alliance of Coaches (APAC) Coaching Fiesta at the beginning of December. That is when I started to recognise that people were really responding to this particular set of concepts. Concepts which for me are always about making the complex simple and turning it into practical action. I want to make it really accessible for people so they do not just hear about it, but they can actually use it and make a difference for themselves.

What I realised following the APAC event was that I really needed to share this with my own tribe. I had not even realised that I had only shared these ideas with tribes beyond my own.

In mid-January, I ran another event and shared the ideas with my own tribe. That garnered even more great responses, personalised emails, and LinkedIn messages, telling me about the impact and the importance of what people had learned during the events, and how it had really helped them to find focus and a way forward in 2021.

A few days later I was in the middle of a conversation and I realised that I needed to turn these concepts into an easy to read book to make the ideas accessible for even more people. So more people could have the opportunity to gain the knowledge and the skills to be able to support themselves, to create a sustainable way of being able to first lead themselves, to enable them to show up right now.

The world needs leadership right now. Anything that you can do to support your own leadership is going to benefit not only you, but also the people and the world around you.

So here I am, 10 days later, adding the finishing touches to this book for you. It isn't perfect. More importantly, it is done and you are reading it right now.

In this book I am going to share with you 5 key concepts that are about setting you up for sustainable, effective, successful leadership. So that you are positioning yourself in a way that is supportable, and making sure that you have the resources to call on so that you can show up as a leader in '21. And, of course, beyond – these concepts are going to be valuable into the future.

This is a quick read. No major stories, no extensive background material. I've done the work for you behind the scenes and taken various complex ideas, theories, research and themes from 2020, and distilled them into 5 simple and easy to implement principles that you can use straightaway. This book is straight to the point so you can get on with supporting yourself and your leadership of self now.

As with everything, though, it's not just about the reading and knowing; it's about the doing. There is a range of activities in this book for you to complete. I encourage you to take one or more of these principles and turn them into action. I know that even one will make a difference for you.

I wish you well, and I'd love to hear from you about the difference it makes.

CHAPTER 1

GET READY

In this book, I am again focused on leading possibility, and in particular, how to first lead yourself. As leaders we have such a big role to play, not just to lead, but also to role model leadership. And I think in these changing conditions, in the world that we're living in with all its complications and complexities, it's important that people can actually see leadership in action. Then they can choose who to follow and who they can emulate, and they can aspire to, and see, what works in terms of leadership practice.

I'm going to start by providing you with some leadership frames, to give you a context in which I'm going to be talking about leadership. For those who have read *First Lead Yourself*, these will be familiar. Then I'm going to share with you 5 key principles to help you to first lead yourself – principles that will help you to build simple and sustainable foundations for leadership success in 2021 and beyond.

Firstly, I think it's really important to recognise that 2021 is not a clean slate. We each need to recognise that a range of challenges that arose in 2020 will be continuing, with more to follow. Added to that, we have a whole lot of people who, although they might have had a break, are still suffering from some fatigue, still carrying some surge capacity depletion. With this in mind, it is essential that as a leader you are looking after yourself and your people.

The world is crying out for leadership, so you also need to be creating a pathway forward that offers your people a level of certainty and stability. People need to be able to trust in your leadership and in you to lead them.

What I want you to think about right now, so you can get the most out of this book, is what feeling you need to bring to really maximise and optimise your reading and this opportunity. It might be curiosity; it might be focus. It might be positive intention, or intent to follow through. Or any one of a hundred other feelings.

ACTIVITY

What is the feeling you need to bring as you read this book?

Write it down here _____

_____

CHAPTER 2

THE MODEL

To give you a little context, what I want to do is share with you how I think about leadership. There are 3 foundation dimensions of leadership.

Of course, the first one is yourself. And that's where I am going to focus this book. There is your tribe, all the people around you. And there is your world, which is the ecosystem in which you operate. That is, all the processes and systems and culture and policies and so on. When you have those 3 dimensions of leadership in your focus, you create the opportunity to inspire, to influence and to have impact. And when you are doing all of those things, that gives you the opportunity to be Leading Possibility.

Leading Possibility™

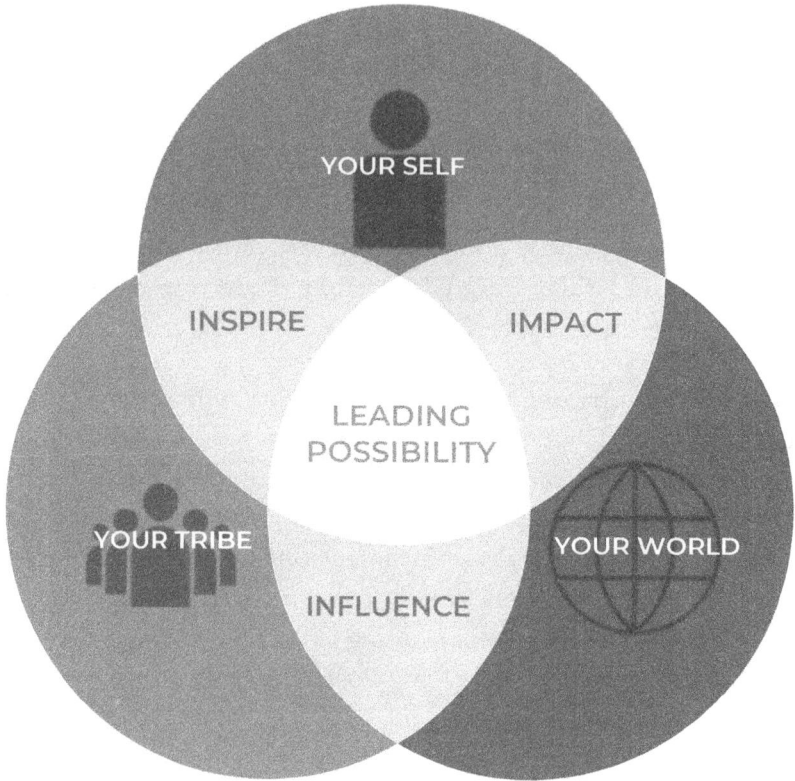

Leading Possibility is not simply going through the motions of leadership; it is about creating legacy. It is about always having a focus on opportunity, what can be and what is possible.

In particular, what I am going to focus on in this book is your leadership of self. I'll be sharing some ideas about how it is that you can really step into your leadership so that you are knowing and being and doing leadership. You will be role modelling leadership for others, and you will also be providing your people with the stability and the certainty that you are leading. They can see it; they can see you as leadership in action. And that is such a key thing at the moment. Everybody is craving leadership.

This has been a big theme through 2020, the need for leadership and for leaders. I think 2021 is going to be more of the same. 2020 brought in a huge portfolio of change that was unexpected and everyone was very reactive, certainly early on. I look at 2020 as the sprint. I think 2021 is the beginning of the marathon of transformation, a new world, a new world of work, a new way of operating, both within and outside of work, because we are faced with a different set of conditions.

We all need to look at how we stay relevant as leaders, and also as businesses. This means things have to change. What was relevant in 2019 is not relevant, necessarily, in 2021. And so we have to be able to lead the longer term change and transformation. That requires sustainable leadership practice.

So let's start with the foundation, and focus in particular on leading yourself. There are 3 key things that you need to be thinking about, reflecting on and taking action on when you consider your own leadership. This is the knowing, being and doing of your personal leadership. And the first thing is that you need to Face Up. And that means you need to look in the mirror pretty regularly and just notice the good, the bad and the ugly. Whatever that may be, simply notice it. This is about elevating your self-awareness.

The second thing you need to do, knowing yourself, is to Show Up with your resources in their fullness as much of the time as you can. This is not about being perfect; it is understanding what your strengths are. It is being mindful and present. You need to show up at your best using your different capacities and capability as much as you can. And that's self-management.

The final component is that you need to Step Up. Step up is about your growth as a leader, and continuously learning so you always have something new to offer the people you serve. It is about self-development.

First Lead Yourself™

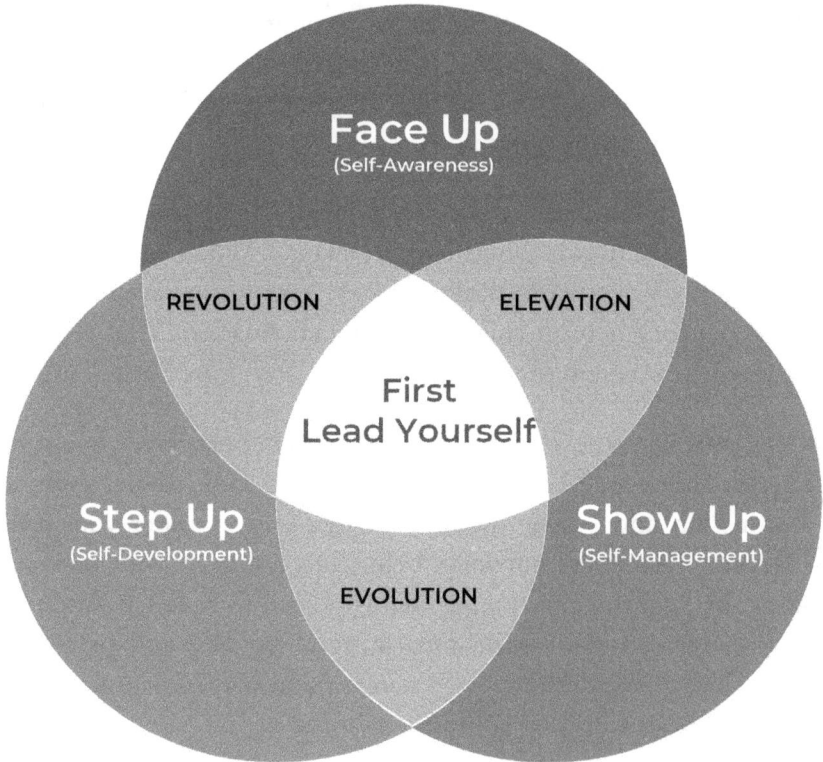

These elements are fundamental to being a leader, to that real commitment to your own leadership, and to the practice of your own leadership. You support the elevation of your leadership, an evolution of your leadership, and finally, a revolution of your leadership. This is the First Lead Yourself philosophy.

This is our focus. You and your leadership of self. In this book, I am primarily focused on helping you to Show Up in 2021 and beyond.

I will share with you 5 key principles that will help you to elevate your leadership right now. To help you to be your best using the resources and strengths you already have. To Show Up in 2021... and beyond.

CHAPTER 3

THE PRINCIPLES

Along with the 5 key principles, I'll share some simple insights into what you can do to first lead yourself and create the opportunity to really step into your leadership and 2021.

The 5 Principles:

1. Fill your own cup.
   As the saying goes, you can't pour from an empty cup. So it is really important that you focus on keeping yourself in the best state possible. So fill your own cup.

2. Foster connection.
   This was a big theme for 2020, that people feel a loss of connection with certain parts of their network and social network. This is key.

3. Focus specifically on the important.
   Which good leaders in emergency do very well.

4. Elevate your practice of leadership.
   Be deliberate about how you develop your leadership.

5. Operate in your zone of genius.
   Fulfil your leadership role using your unique strengths, knowledge and skills.

CHAPTER 4

PRINCIPLE 1: FILL YOUR OWN CUP

W hy is this important? Because leaders have had a challenging year, and there is more ahead. Leaders are fatigued, yet know they need to show up for themselves, their teams and their organisations. Leaders need to look after themselves, so they can look after others.

I'm sharing with you a simple exercise designed to help you fill your own cup. You might want to grab a pen and paper or tablet, whatever you use to take your notes. This is going to be based on the wheels of life, which you may be familiar with. It is about understanding, when you think about your need to fill your own cup, what for you are the things that bring you energy. The things that really do fill your cup.

This is about identifying the things that you need to have in place to support you, the factors that influence how able you are as a leader. The things that influence how resourced you feel, how resilient you feel, how energetic you feel, how focused you feel. What are the things that you absolutely need in order to be operating at your best?

ACTIVITY

So start by drawing this wheel (or download the resources for this book to get the template https://ashleycoaching. com.au/show-up21-resources/).

Draw a big circle, and then you'll be putting some dimensions in it. I typically put in about 8 dimensions. You might have more, or you might have slightly less. Perhaps you'll have 6 or 10, something like that. Draw your wheel with spokes for your different factors.

Wheel of Success

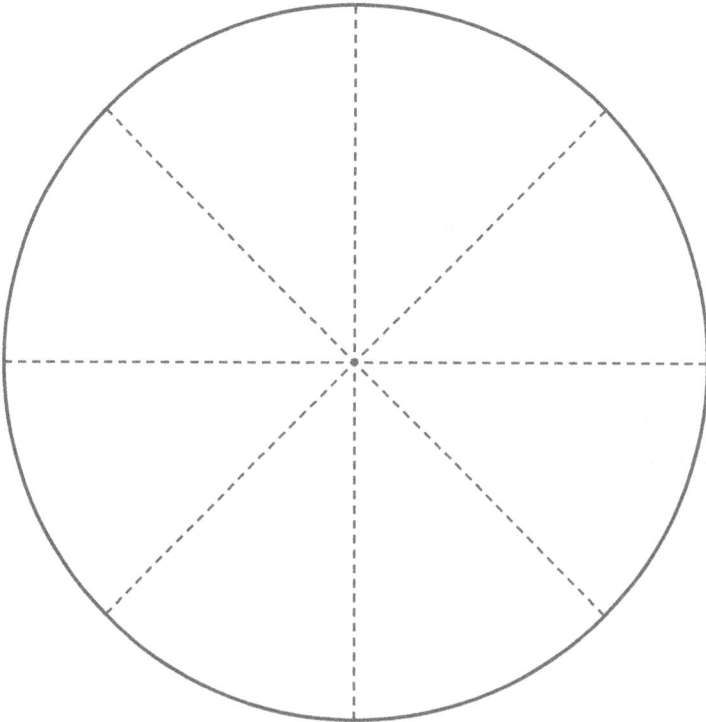

And now I'll walk you through the factors.

They are going to be different for everyone. Some of the key factors for me, and you can just fill out your wheel as we go, are things like sleep – super important. When you're sleep deprived, you don't make good decisions, which is not great for a leader. So sleep, how you do food that works for you, exercise. And then from there you'll probably have different factors. For me, there's a family piece that needs to happen, there's social stuff that I need to have going on. If I don't have that, I'm not at my best.

I like to get outside – that's really key for me. If I don't get outside, I'll start to feel a bit flat after a while. And so on. Also, reading is important to me and learning is important to me.

You will have different things. Some people have meditation or yoga, or crafting, or what else? They might have prayer. There is a whole gamut of things. This is about what is important to you. What are the factors that when you have that, or you're doing that, or you are spending time in that, it really helps to build your energy and your resources?

ACTIVITY

Please fill out your factors on your wheel, just like my example on the next page…with your unique factors that bring you energy.

Now you are going to complete a quick self-assessment for each of your factors, within the range of 0 to 10, with 0 in the middle and 10 on the outside. It's important to note that you don't necessarily need to have a factor at 10 for it to be filling your cup. You may not ever get 10 and that's fine.

ACTIVITY

Now I want you to ask yourself and assess: Where am I operating right now? And as I said, you don't necessarily need to get to 10 for a factor to be enough to be resourcing you. You make an estimate of each of those elements right now, and then you join them up. You will end up with kind of a wonky wheel, like mine below.

Wheel of Success

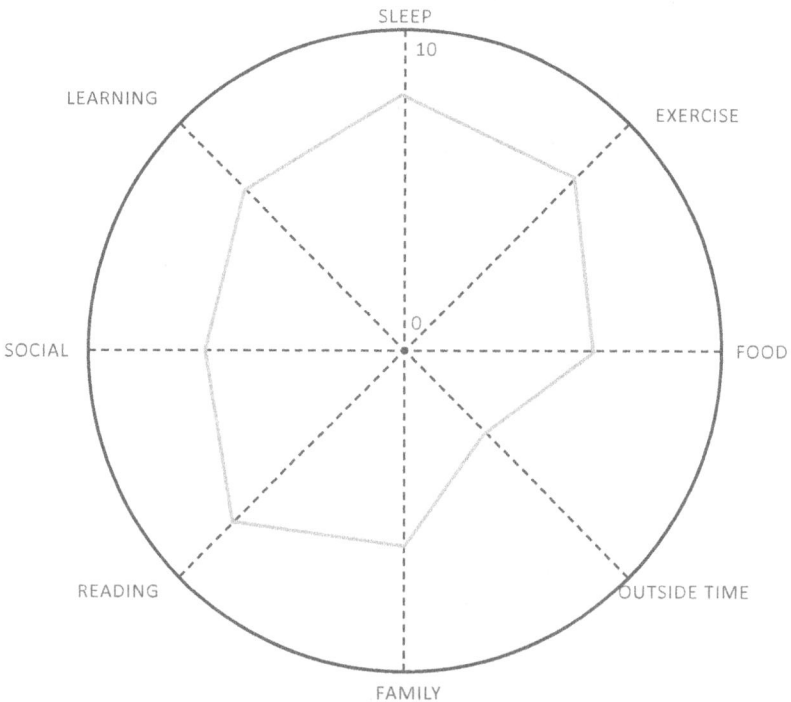

I would say sleep is pretty good for me. Food is average. Exercise is good. Family is okay. Outside time, not great. Reading is good. Learning, okay. So again, self-assess really quickly where you are right now, and then just join up those points. And you will get a wonky wheel, something like mine. The idea here is to understand what is going on for you at the moment and how that is supporting you.

Consider yourself right now.

- How are you feeling?
- How full is your cup?

Now consider your wheel. Some things might come to mind already as opportunities or some of the contributing factors as to why you're feeling like you're feeling.

You might be feeling great because you're getting a little bit of everything you need. Or you might be feeling a little bit flat, or unmotivated, or something like that. And there might be something here that could help you with that.

ACTIVITY

Let's move to the next step. Pick a different colour to draw with.

Now look at your wheel and consider: Where would I like these different factors to be so that I really am filling my cup? So I'm feeling resourced? So I'm feeling capable? So I'm ready to lead in 2021?

For me on my wheel, sleep is already good, food is okay, exercise could help, some more outside time would definitely help the way I feel. Family is good. A little bit more reading and learning would be nice.

And so again, join up your points. And you'll get a different wonky wheel this time. Most people do. It's unusual, in my experience, that someone has got everything exactly where they would like it to be.

Wheel of Success

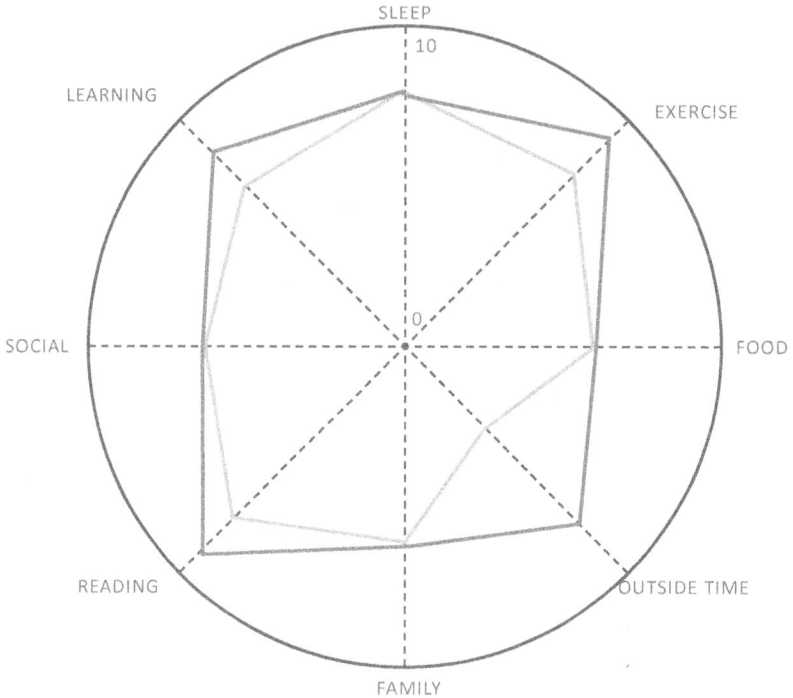

What you will notice is that between your first wheel where you are, and your second wheel, where you'd like to be, there are some smaller spaces, and there are some bigger spaces, and that's where your opportunity is to really fill your cup.

For me, I have outside time as my big opportunity. Also exercise, reading and learning have a smaller opportunity.

Wheel of Success

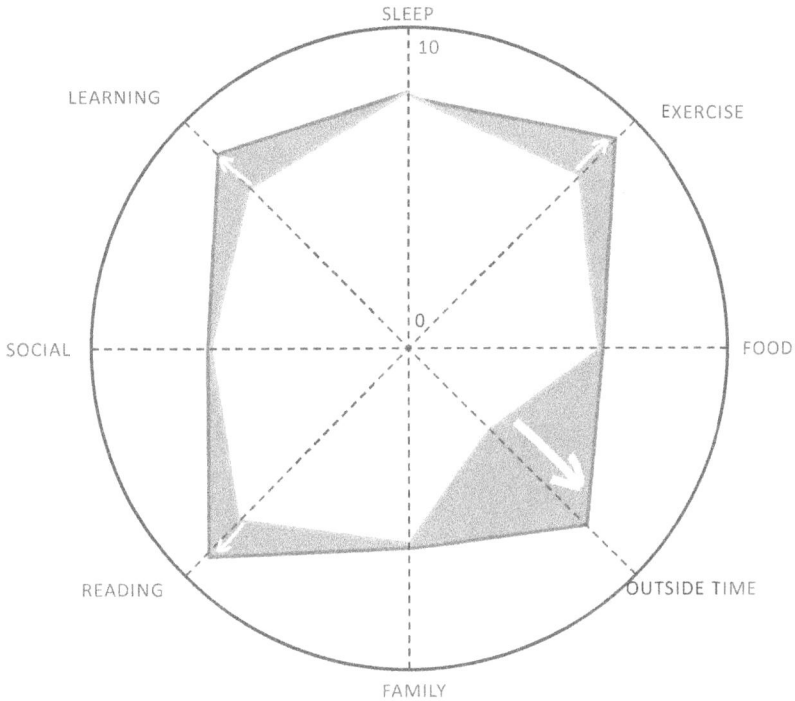

Now, knowing that, I can choose to take some action. I could choose to get some outside time. Perhaps I'll go for a couple of walks each week on the beach. That will also help my exercise. And I can create some learning opportunity for myself, whatever it is that I choose to do.

ACTIVITY

You can do exactly the same thing for yourself.

- What are the one or two big gaps on your wheel that would really help to resource you?

- And what do you choose to do about that?

It's a little bit of self-coaching, which is, of course, such a key when we are first leading ourselves.

You can then follow that through.

- What are you going to do?
- When are you going to do it?
- What are the steps?
- By what date?
- What is the commitment you're making?
- Who are you going to share it with?

ACTIVITY

Ask yourself these questions so that you know you really have a follow through process. Now pop it into your calendar, or whatever other commitment you need to make, in order to hold yourself accountable to filling your own cup.

That was Principle 1, which was about helping you to fill your own cup.

CHAPTER 5

PRINCIPLE 2: FOSTER CONNECTION

The second thing I want to talk about is the importance of connection. It was a really interesting year in 2020 because a lot of people have reported that their connection with family improved, due to a lot of people working from home. They were seeing more of their family and spending more time with them. And that's a wonderful outcome.

On the other hand, though, there is a range of research showing some other outcomes. Research from Glint's employee engagement data in August 2020 found that more than 30% of people felt that they were less connected with their teams than they had been in 2019. And more than 35% of people feel that they are less connected with their leaders than they were in 2019. That is not ideal. This is consistent with the stories I am hearing from the leaders I work with.

Leaders want people to feel connected, to feel part of the community at work in terms of both their team and their business. People who feel more connected are typically more engaged and more productive. Therefore, it is an area that we need to really be conscious of. It has an impact.

Another thing that makes this important is that people who are connected, who have a network that extends both within their organisation and outside the organisation, are generally happier, they are more productive, they are high performing, they get paid more, they get promoted more often and they are better liked.

As a leader and an influencer, if you have a strong network, it helps you to access information, to have a support structure around you, to be higher performing, to be more productive, to be more effective and to reap the rewards of that in terms of job opportunities and so on.

So, what I want to share with you are some ideas to think about in terms of getting a supportive network around you. Creating connection for yourself. These are based on the work of Robin Dunbar, an evolutionary anthropologist. This is what he determined in relation to the numbers of people that humans work effectively with in their tribes, and the numbers they are able to cope with cognitively.

We start with your inner circle, the 5 closest relationships.

And those 5, they might be family members, or they may not be. They might include, for example, a trusted long-term mentor. Beyond that inner circle, and very important for leaders, is the circle of 15. There are 15 key relationships that everybody has. The 15 really strong, robust relationships that become their core go-to people, and the core people that they also support. The people who have real impact and influence on your success.

Dunbar's Number

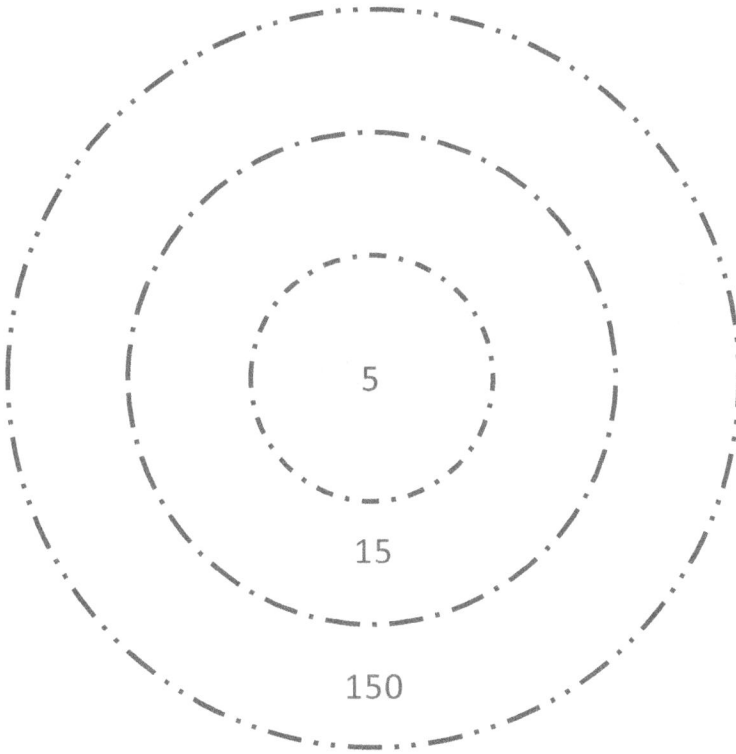

5

15

150

So the question is, who makes up that 15 for you?

It could be peers, team members, teachers, your leader. It could be partners, customers or stakeholders. Perhaps it includes industry peers or mentors. These people could come from anywhere. But it's up to you to think about: Who are those 15 super relationships I want to have?

Key Relationships

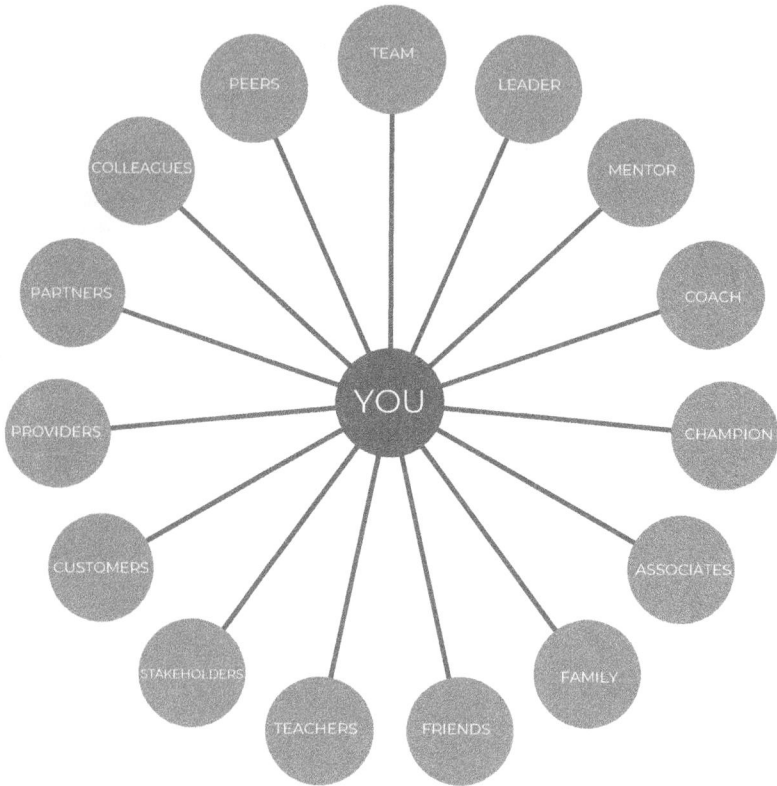

These are the people who really get you. They are also the people you really want to be able to help and support, as well as them helping and supporting you. These are the make-or-break characters in terms of your network.

- I want you to really consider who is in that 15 right now.
- How well is each relationship working right now?
- Who else needs to be in that 15 for this year?

Beyond that, you have a circle of 150 people. You are not as invested in these relationships as in your 5 and 15, though they are still important. 150 is the number that we can manage effectively.

For our purposes, and to set yourself up for sustainable leadership, let's focus on the 15. This is the number that I want you to think about for fostering connection.

- What is the state of your 15 important relationships?
- And what do you need to do about that?
- How are they supporting you?
- How are you supporting them?
- How recently have you had contact with these 15 people?

The conditions of 2020 changed things. Some relationships didn't receive attention. That's okay, people do understand it was a strange year. It's now about being proactive and getting your key 15 back into focus. It's time to think about who is in that group and what you need to do to make sure that the relationship is supporting you both. And that's not about getting on the phone for half an hour with every person, every week or anything like that. You will know what's needed to keep the relationship current.

ACTIVITY

Right now, brainstorm your key 15 people.

I talk to my clients about relationships in 3 tiers.

There are the hot zone relationships, the ones you're super invested in, put a lot of energy and focus into. Think in terms of your inner circle of 5.

There are the warm zone relationships, which you do invest in, but not quite as much. You don't put in as much of your attention or as much of your focus, but you do continue to nurture them because they are important. These are your key 15.

And then there are the lukewarm relationships where they are perhaps people that you have known in the past, though right now they are not as relevant, yet you keep in occasional contact with. Or they are people that you have on your radar, but you haven't really initiated the relationship with yet, or you haven't elevated into the warm or hot status yet. These are your circle of 150 relationships.

Relationship Heat Map

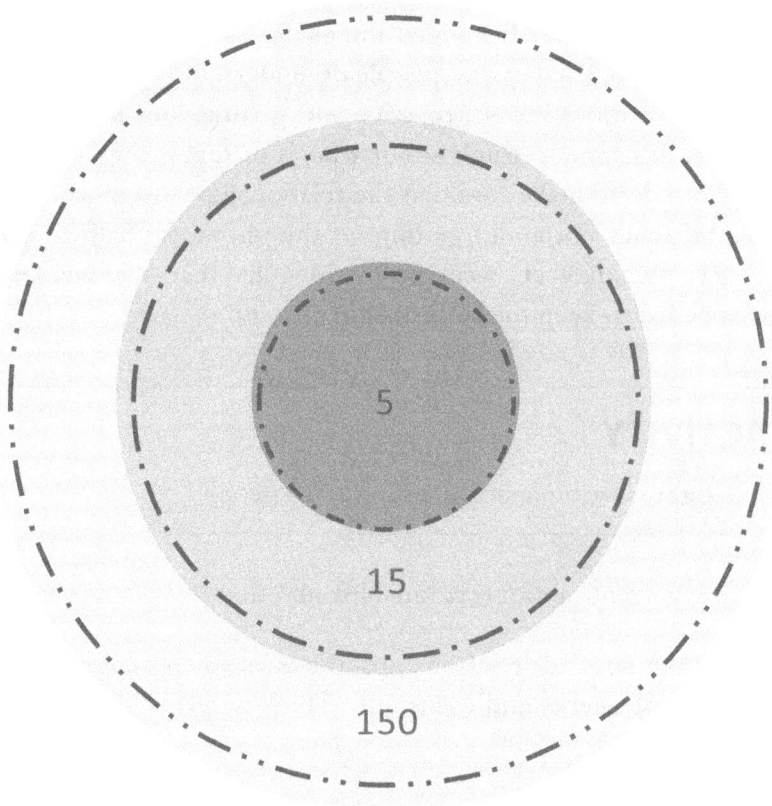

Some things to think about:

- Are you making good relationship choices for yourself in terms of what you need as a leader?
- How comfortable do you feel that you have the right kind of network?
- How well is your network working for you?
- How well are you working for your network?
- What actions do you need to take here to make sure you have your network layered in the lukewarm, warm and hot zones and aligning with your 5, 15 and 150 circle?

CHAPTER 6

PRINCIPLE 3: FOCUS SPECIFICALLY ON THE IMPORTANT

T he third principle, to focus specifically on the important, came up for me because I've done a lot of work as a productivity consultant over the years, and looked at what helps people to be high performers. And last year I did a lot of research in the area of leadership during emergency and disaster situations. The clear theme in both these areas is that good leadership means leaders only focus specifically on the important – where they can add value and make an impact.

They don't get caught up in the noise. They don't get caught up in busy work. They don't get distracted. They focus specifically and only on the important.

This means, as leaders, being very conscious about the choices we make. Where do you put your attention, your energy and your focus? You may be familiar with the Time Management Matrix, which is a Stephen Covey model, as a way of understanding the different types of work and where you should put your focus for maximum effect.

There are two things to think about. If you want to be making the biggest difference you can as a leader, regardless of the conditions, or even in perfect conditions, rather than pandemic conditions, do not just consider urgency when you make decisions about what to work on. You also need to consider impact.

So we have an urgency factor, and we have an impact factor. And when I say impact, I mean, how important is this work? What value does it add? We have high impact and low impact on the vertical axis. And we have very urgent and not yet urgent on the horizontal axis. And so we get these four quadrants of different combinations of urgency and impact.

Time Management Matrix (TMM)

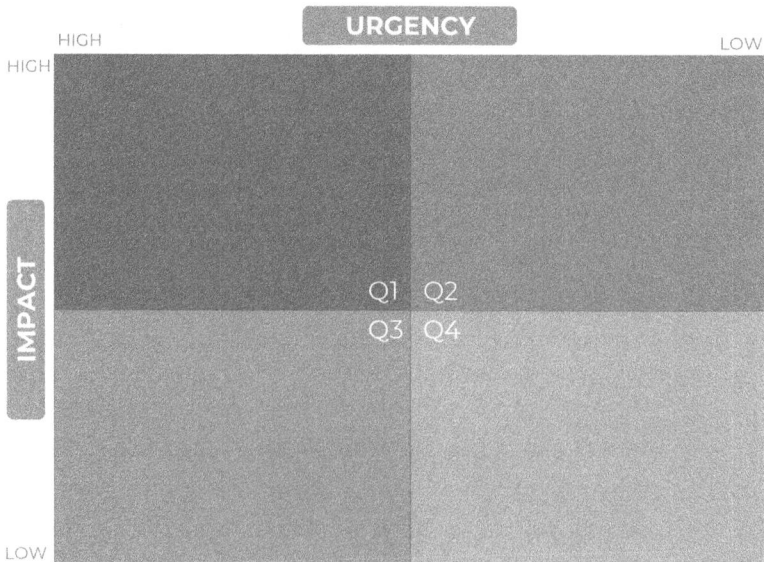

Adapted from Stephen Covey's "First Things First" Covey Leadership Center, Inc © 2003

In summary, as leaders, you want to be operating above the horizontal midline in Quadrants 1 and 2. You want everything you do to be about high impact. You don't want it to be low impact. It is not a good use of your time. You are there to make a difference in your role as a leader, so you need to invest yourself in the things that add value. You want to be operating above the line.

TMM — Typical Tasks

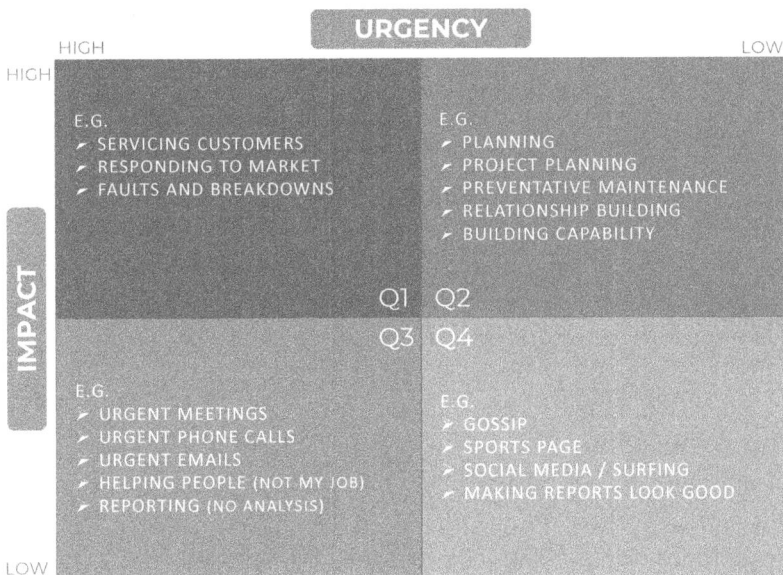

	URGENCY	
	HIGH	LOW
HIGH	E.G.	E.G.
	⟶ SERVICING CUSTOMERS	⟶ PLANNING
	⟶ RESPONDING TO MARKET	⟶ PROJECT PLANNING
	⟶ FAULTS AND BREAKDOWNS	⟶ PREVENTATIVE MAINTENANCE
		⟶ RELATIONSHIP BUILDING
		⟶ BUILDING CAPABILITY
IMPACT	Q1	Q2
	Q3	Q4
	E.G.	E.G.
	⟶ URGENT MEETINGS	⟶ GOSSIP
	⟶ URGENT PHONE CALLS	⟶ SPORTS PAGE
	⟶ URGENT EMAILS	⟶ SOCIAL MEDIA / SURFING
	⟶ HELPING PEOPLE (NOT MY JOB)	⟶ MAKING REPORTS LOOK GOOD
LOW	⟶ REPORTING (NO ANALYSIS)	

Adapted from Stephen Covey's "First Things First" Covey Leadership Center, Inc © 2003

To give you an example, this Quadrant 3, which is below the line, is low impact and urgent. This is busy work. You must attend this meeting, you have to take this phone call, you need to do this report, which no one will ever look at. It's busy work. It makes no difference. And yet there is this real adrenaline thing that goes on there. If you stay in Quadrant 3, you tick off your very long to-do list and yet, when you get to the end of the day, you wonder: What did I achieve today?

Yes, I ticked off my list, but what difference did it make?

You know what? It didn't actually make a big difference.

Focus your limited time, energy, effort and attention on important things. Think about yourself as this incredibly valuable asset. You need to invest yourself wisely to make that difference. And so invest yourself in the high impact.

When you get new things coming into your space, consider:

- How important is this?
- Why should I be doing this?
- What makes it important?

Challenge. Ask those questions.

Your objective is to be spending no more than about 25% of your time, hopefully less, in the 'it is highly impactful' and 'it is urgent' Quadrant 1.

This includes things like something broke, and we need to fix it. It's things like a customer needs something urgently. It's not in the normal delivery space, something went wrong, we need to fix it for our customer. It could be market conditions changed, we've got to urgently respond to that. It could be we've got a pandemic, we have to respond to that. That's your important and urgent.

Quadrant 2 is important, and it is not yet urgent. This is the stuff you plan and complete. So you have, for example, a customer supply chain. It doesn't go into Quadrant 1 because we know how to do it. And we plan it, and we complete it, and we deliver it on time, most of the time. When there is a problem with it, that's Quadrant 1.

So Quadrant 2 is about plan and complete. This includes project planning, business planning, strategic planning – all of that goes in there.

It is also about prevention of problems. So preventative maintenance. And that could be preventative maintenance on systems, processes, technology, people. It's making sure your people go on holidays, or have health and well-being support, all that kind of stuff goes in there.

Relationship building is another one that goes in Quadrant 2. That is right up there with what I've just talked about in terms of your network, your connectivity, having that support structure around you. And that is both within your team and organisation, but also beyond your organisation.

There is considerable research to evidence that people who have a network that extends beyond their current organisation actually have a more positive mindset and are high performing (iOpener Institute). So you want relationship building to be something that you focus on.

And then the final thing that I want to include here is capability building or development. And again, that's technology, and it is also people. You need to be building capability for the future. You need to invest in your people to develop them so that they can do all the great stuff that you have planned. And so that you remain relevant.

TMM Your Target Focus

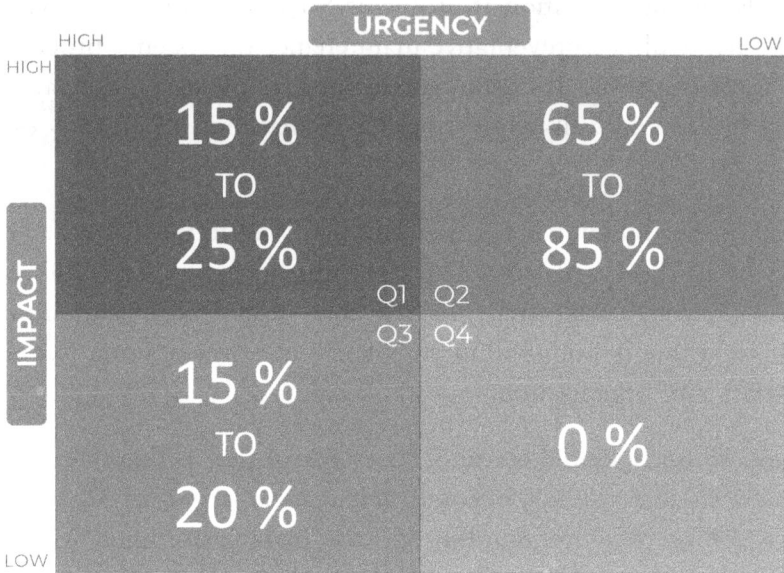

| | URGENCY | |
| HIGH | | LOW |

HIGH

IMPACT

15 % TO 25 % Q1	Q2 65 % TO 85 %
Q3	Q4
15 % TO 20 %	0 %

LOW

I'm up in the upper right quadrant of the Time Management Matrix. To give you a sense, the highest performers spend 65% to 85% of their time in this quadrant. A high impact, value adding activity that is not yet urgent, focusing on the specifically important. When you think about your calendar, and you think about what you are going to commit time to, it should primarily be Quadrant 2 activity. You need to be clear about the decisions you make so that you are focused on the specifically important.

Yes, you will do some Quadrant 1, and you allow some time to react to Quadrant 1, because we know we always have Quadrant 1. So allow a bit of time each day for that. Do not fill up your calendar with Quadrant 2; allow some space to react. In terms of where to focus, if you want to be first leading yourself, you need to focus on those activities where you make the biggest difference. Which is high impact, value adding activity.

So when you think about your planning, think about how you are spending your time, and how you choose what you are going to focus on. Remember the importance of focusing on the important.

Now, personally, every Friday afternoon I look at the week ahead and I make those choices. Of course, I've got time booked out weeks and weeks in advance. But I specifically look at the next week or two to make sure that I am focused on the important and the impactful.

ACTIVITY

Complete the Time Management Matrix for yourself.

- Where are you spending your time right now? Which quadrants?

- What action do you need to take to ensure you focus specifically on the important?

- How do you plan to stay focused on the important moving forwards?

CHAPTER 7

PRINCIPLE 4: ELEVATE YOUR PRACTICE

There are two simple ideas I want to share with you to help you elevate your practice. Before I do that, though, very quickly just consider that leadership is a practice. It is something that we need to work on in order to improve. Being a leader does not happen simply because we want it to, or because we end up in a leadership role. Real leaders continue to learn, to apply and activate their learning, and in doing so add more to their leadership. They practise leadership.

Feedback

The first idea to elevate your practice of leadership is to be proactive about getting feedback, actively eliciting feedback from people. Something we can all be better at is getting more feedback, and getting more of the right sort of feedback so that it really contributes to you elevating your practice.

To improve the quality of the feedback you receive, I suggest asking very specific questions rather than general questions. Asking general questions like 'What do you think of my leadership?' will get you general answers like 'It's fine.' Which doesn't help you very much.

Asking specific questions like 'What one thing could I improve in my leadership approach?' is likely to elicit a more specific and valuable response. A response which you can then choose to turn into action.

The other suggestion I have for eliciting useful feedback is to use an above-the-line approach, which helps people to feel comfortable about offering you feedback.

Firstly, you can ask someone, 'What went well?'

For example, 'What went well in today's presentation?' People are comfortable offering some positive observations to start the conversation. This does not typically provide you with an opportunity for improvement, though. So we need part two of this conversation.

You can follow up by asking the other person to complete this statement: 'It would be even better if…'

That provides an opportunity for them to share ideas and suggestions for improvement in a constructive way. Much more comfortable.

Try it out next time you want some useful feedback.

WWW EBI

WHAT   **E**VEN

WENT  **B**ETTER

WELL **?**   **I**F

Space to Lead

The second idea to help you elevate your practice of leadership is to create the space to lead.

There are 3 elements to consider here. I have already discussed the idea of specifically focusing only on the important. In order to be able to do that, though, you need the right conditions to be able to focus, so that you can be leading and elevating your practice of leadership.

The first element here to create the space to lead is to consider your physical environment, the space that you work in.

- Is it a space that is conducive to supporting your work? Or is it messy and cluttered?

- Have you got enough space?
- Have you got the right kind of equipment?
- Can you find the things you need for your work?

The second thing is the calendar space, and I have mentioned a little about this earlier in the book.

- Have you got time to do the important work?
- Have you allocated time to do the important work? Or is your calendar full of meetings that add no value?

The third element is your mental space.

- Have you got any mental space or is your brain cluttered full of junk?
- Are you trying to remember your to-do list?
- Are you stressing about something else that you have not taken control of?

Start thinking about your mental space as well.

You need to clean out those 3 spaces so that you do have the space to lead, which enables you to generate the potential to focus, to think and to create as a leader.

Space to Lead

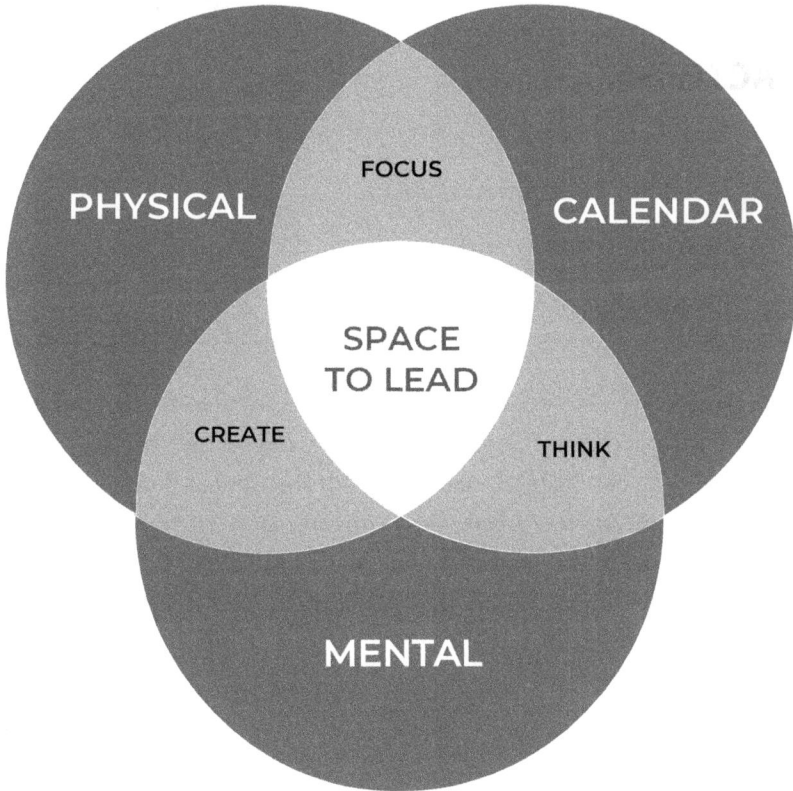

There are many things that you can do to support this.

High priorities should be decluttering your work environment, whether you are working from home or in the office. Decluttering your calendar and making sure that only the important things go into your calendar. Decluttering your brain. If you have things you need to remember, put them somewhere else, for example, on a to-do list or in your calendar. Somewhere that is not your brain. You can only hold about 7 thoughts consciously at the same time. So if you have more than that, they're competing for space. Declutter is the key idea here.

> **ACTIVITY**
>
> Just do it.
>
> Declutter your physical space.
>
> Declutter your calendar space.
>
> Declutter your mental space.

Then you create that space for you to step into your leadership, to elevate your practice of leadership, because you can think, you can focus and you can create. And creativity is such a key activity for leaders. It is about new ideas, new options, new choices. It is about vision, it is about the structure of team and capability, it is about process improvement, all of this is creative. You need the space to create and be strategic.

CHAPTER 8

PRINCIPLE 5: YOUR ZONE OF GENIUS

O perate in your zone of genius. What I mean is to get in flow, to be in the space where things are easy for you. The space where you are using your strengths and you are using your energy, and you are doing things with ease.

When we think about ourselves as leaders, obviously we want to invest ourselves in the important, we want to have a nice, great space to be able to work in, we want to resource ourselves. But we also want to get into that zone where things are just easier. I'm sure you have done work and it's just been hard. It has drained you of energy, maybe it was boring, or it feels like you go at a snail's pace and you don't make a lot of progress. Often it feels like that because you are working outside your zone of genius.

Think about your current situation.

- How much of your time are you currently spending in your zone of genius?
- How do you spend as much time as possible in your zone of genius?
- How do you even find your zone of genius?

The first thing is to ask yourself these 3 questions:

1. What do I know?
   Which is skills, experience, capability, everything you have learned.

2. What do I love?
   What brings me energy? What makes me happy? What gives me satisfaction? What do I feel really enthused about? Where am I using my strengths? That sort of thing.

3. And then, how can I contribute?
   The contribution is about: What are the goals for myself, my team, my business? What is the vision? What is the mission? So where can I contribute to that?

That creates the potential for you to be productive, as you use your knowledge and skills to contribute, and to have passion for what you are doing, because you know it and you love it. And to be on purpose, because you are contributing to a space that you love and enjoy, and you are using your strengths.

This is your zone of genius. Your potential.

Know, Love, Contribute™

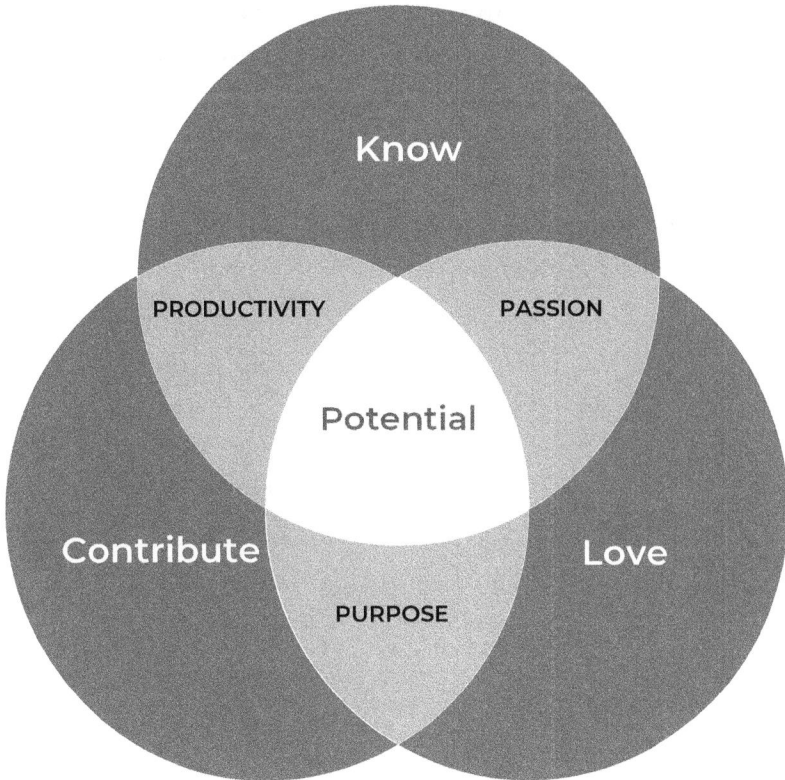

ACTIVITY

The next step is to really think about those key things for yourself. This is a straightforward brainstorming exercise. I'd really encourage you to think about these questions for yourself and capture your ideas. Make a list or a mind map.

- What are all the things I know? My skills, experiences, learning, knowledge.

- What are all the things I love that bring me energy? And that could be talking to people, it could be going through information, it could be working in teams, it could be making decisions, teaching others, building relationships, detail, strategy. There are so many things.

- How can I contribute to the bigger picture? Again, this is about the impact, high impact, high value adding.

When you bring those 3 things together, you get into that zone of genius where you can get into your peak flow state and things happen. And this does not drain your energy, but instead it brings you energy and you make a big contribution. You are using all of the great knowledge and skills you have accumulated over the course of your life.

If you operate in this space as much of the time as you can, you will be making a contribution, you will be focused on the important, and you will be supporting your resourcefulness. You are not working against yourself – you are working with yourself. And this makes it easier to maintain your cup at a higher level of full because you are not doing things that drain your energy.

If you can apply these ideas and look for the opportunities in your role as a leader to really be able to bring those things together in your zone of genius, life is going to be so much easier. There are enough complications in the world, simply with the rate of change. Forget the pandemic. Just the rate of change, technological advancement, the real interconnectivity, the speed at which everything happens, and then put a global pandemic on top – we've got enough complexity. Make it easy for yourself to lead by being in your zone of genius.

ACTIVITY

Consider what you can do to operate more often in your zone of genius.

CHAPTER 9

SHOW UP

So these are my 5 key principles to help you Show Up and some ideas to first lead yourself. If you choose any one of these and make some progress, I'll be happy. Any more than that, I'll be over the moon because I know you will be better positioned for sustainable leadership.

So Show Up. Take action that will support you and your leadership and rise to the challenge.

Good luck.

I'd love to know how you go.

ACKNOWLEDGEMENTS

A few quick thoughts, as time is of the essence. I want to get this book out to you as soon as I can so you can take the action you need to.

For their ongoing inspiration and support, the Inspirational Book Writing team. Your help and guidance is always valuable and so greatly appreciated. Book number 3, so I guess I really am an author now.

To Sylvie and the team at bookpod.com, I am grateful for your support and speedy turnaround to help me bring this book to fruition so quickly.

To my family, a big thank you for putting up with my single-minded focus.

And to my tremendous colleagues and clients, I value your input, your challenge and your ideas so much.

ABOUT THE AUTHOR

STACEY ASHLEY IS A LEADERSHIP AND COACHING EXPERT.

Obsessed with possibility, Stacey helps leaders to navigate the complexities of globalisation, technological advancement, social interconnectivity, massively accelerating change, and a multi-generational workforce.

With over 30 years' experience, Stacey has helped thousands to develop their leadership competence, confidence and credibility. The author of Amazon #1 best seller *The New Leader*, she has been featured in *The Age*, *Sydney Morning Herald*, INTHEBLACK, HRD, *CEO Magazine* & *Coaching World*. She typically speaks at conferences, runs workshops, consults and coaches.

She helps HRDs, People & Culture Executives, C Suite, Executives, Transformation & Change Leaders:

- ✔ Build the practical foundations for effective leadership
- ✔ Get out of the trenches, to lead strategically and with influence
- ✔ Transition quickly and effectively to leading larger, more complex portfolios
- ✔ Effectively lead change and transformation
- ✔ Develop a coaching toolkit and approach
- ✔ Create a leadership coaching capability

Among her many awards:

- LinkedIn Top Voices 2018

- Four International Stevie Awards, including for Coach of the Year 2019

- Nominated Telstra Business & Women's Awards 9 times, including 2020

- Best in Executive Coaching Services – Australia 2019

- Most Influential Woman in Executive Coaching 2020 – Australia

Stacey's clients include: ABC, ASX, AAPT, ACCOR Hotels, AEC, ANU, CBA, CSIRO, DHA, Engie, JORA, MLC, Mustad, Navitas, NDIS, Perrigo, QLD Ed, Torrens Uni, UBank, UNSW, ZIP.

Her clients describe Stacey as calm, personable, visionary, challenging and generous.

Find Stacey Ashley Online

Website
www.staceyashley.com

LinkedIn
https://www.linkedin.com/in/staceyashley/

Facebook
https://www.facebook.com/thestaceyashley/

Instagram
https://www.instagram.com/staceyashleycoaching/

Messenger
m.me/thestaceyashley

Email
stacey@staceyashley.com

Work with Stacey Ashley

To book Stacey Ashley as your speaker visit www.staceyashley.com

For executive coaching visit www.staceyashley.com

Training programs and events visit www.staceyashley.com

SHOW UP²¹ – Bonus Resources:

https://ashleycoaching.com.au/show-up21-resources/

Complimentary Resources:

- 28-Day Self-coaching Challenge, Leadership Performance Boost™

  Visit https://ashleycoaching.com.au/28days

- Complimentary webcast

  Visit https://ashleycoaching.com.au/webcast

Notes

Notes

Notes

Notes

Notes

Notes

www.ingramcontent.com/pod-product-compliance
Lightning Source LLC
Chambersburg PA
CBHW060645210326
41520CB00010B/1750